DIANA KRALL

LIVE IN PARIS

Cover photo by Bruce Weber

ISBN 0-634-06333-2

HAL•LEONARD®
CORPORATION
7777 W. BLUEMOUND RD. P.O. BOX 13819 MILWAUKEE, WI 53213

Visit Hal Leonard Online at
www.halleonard.com

DIANA KRALL

LIVE IN PARIS

CONTENTS

I LOVE BEING HERE WITH YOU

Words and Music by PEGGY LEE
and BILL SCHLUGER

LET'S FALL IN LOVE

Words by TED KOEHLER
Music by HAROLD ARLEN

'DEED I DO

Words and Music by WALTER HIRSCH
and FRED ROSE

THE LOOK OF LOVE

Words by HAL DAVID
Music by BURT BACHARACH

EAST OF THE SUN
(And West of the Moon)

Words and Music by
BROOKS BOWMAN

Slowly, with expression

East of the sun _____ and west of the moon, _____

we'll build a dream - house _____ of love, dear. Near to the sun in the

Up a-mong the stars we'll find, A har-mo-ny of life to a love-ly tune,

east of the sun and west of the moon, dear, east of the sun and

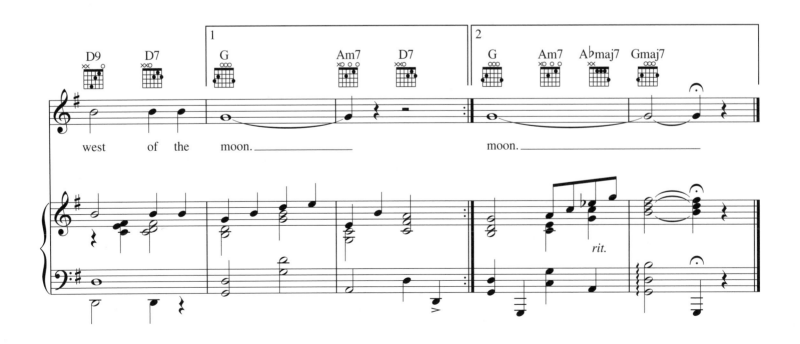

west of the moon._____ moon._____

I'VE GOT YOU UNDER MY SKIN

Words and Music by
COLE PORTER

DEVIL MAY CARE

Words and Music by BOB DOROUGH
and TERRELL P. KIRK, JR.

(1., 3.) No ____ cares for me; I'm ____ hap-py ____
2. *Solos ad lib*

Original key: B♭ minor. This edition has been transposed up one whole step to be more playable.

MAYBE YOU'LL BE THERE

Words by SAMMY GALLOP
Music by RUBE BLOOM

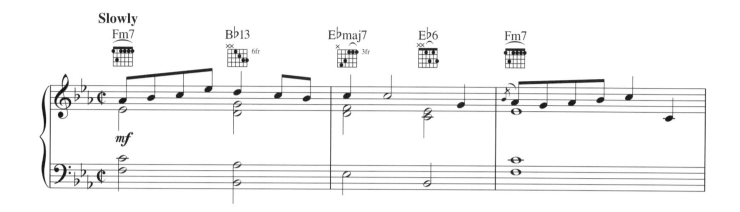

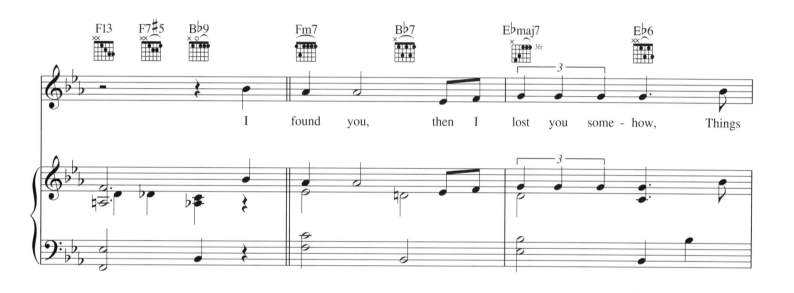

I found you, then I lost you some-how, Things

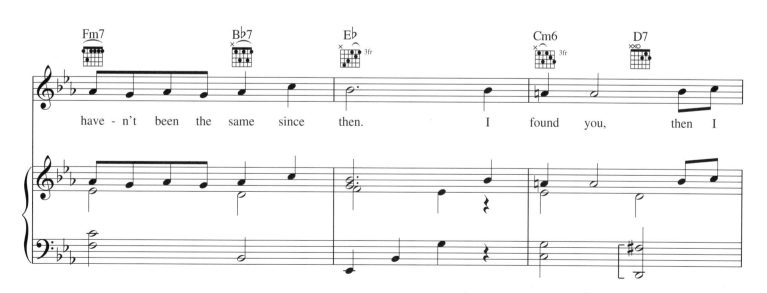

have-n't been the same since then. I found you, then I

'S WONDERFUL

Music and Lyrics by GEORGE GERSHWIN
and IRA GERSHWIN

FLY ME TO THE MOON
(In Other Words)

Words and Music by
BART HOWARD

A CASE OF YOU

Words and Music by
JONI MITCHELL

D. S. al ◆ Coda

part of you pours out of me ___ in these lines ___ from time to time. ___

◆ *Coda*

I met a wom-an. ___ She had ___ a mouth like yours; ___ she knew your life; ___ she knew your dev-

ils and your deeds. ___ And she said "Go ___ to him, stay with him if you can, ___ be pre-pared to

bleed." ___ Oh, but you are in ___ my blood you're my ho - ly wine ___ you're so ___

JUST THE WAY YOU ARE

Words and Music by
BILLY JOEL